STEVENSON'S DR JEKYLL AND MR HYDE

AN AQA ESSAY WRITING GUIDE

R. P. DAVIS

For Monty.

CONTENTS

FOREWORD

In your GCSE English Literature exam, you will be presented with an extract from Robert Louis Stevenson's *The Strange Case of Dr Jekyll and Mr Hyde* and a question that asks you to offer both a close analysis of the extract plus a commentary of the novel as a whole. Of course, there are many methods one *might* use to tackle this style of question. However, there is one particular technique which, due to its sophistication, most readily allows students to unlock the highest marks: namely, **the thematic method**.

To be clear, this study guide is *not* intended to walk you through the novel scene-by-scene: there are many great guides out there that do just that. No, this guide, by sifting through a series of mock exam questions, will demonstrate *how* to organise a response thematically and thus write a stellar essay: a skill we believe no other study guide adequately covers!

I have encountered students who have structured their essays all sorts of ways: some by writing about the extract line by line, others by identifying various language techniques and giving each its own paragraph. The method I'm advocating, on the other hand, involves picking out three to four themes that will allow you to holistically answer the question: these three to four themes will become the three to four content paragraphs of your essay, cushioned between a brief introduction and conclusion. Ideally, these themes will follow from one to the next to create a flowing argument. Within each of these thematic paragraphs, you can then ensure you are jumping through the mark scheme's hoops.

So to break things down further, each thematic paragraph will include various point-scoring components. In each paragraph, you will quote from the extract, offer analyses of these quotes, then discuss how the specific language techniques you have identified illustrate the theme you're discussing. In each paragraph, you will also discuss how other parts of the novel further illustrate the theme (or even complicate it). And in each, you will comment on the era in which the novel was written and how that helps to understand the chosen theme.

Don't worry if this all feels daunting. Throughout this guide, I will be illustrating in great detail – by means of examples – how to build an essay of this kind.

Victoria Road in Edinburgh - just around the corner from Stevenson's childhood home.

The beauty of the thematic approach is that, once you have your themes, you suddenly have a direction and a trajectory, and this makes essay writing a whole lot easier. However, it must also be noted that extracting themes in the first place is something students often find tricky. I have come across many candidates who understand the extract and the novel inside out; but when they are presented with a question under exam conditions, and the pressure kicks in, they find it tough to break their response down into themes. The fact of the matter is: the process is a *creative* one and the best themes require a bit of imagination.

In this guide, I shall take seven different exam-style questions, coupled with extracts from the novel, and put together a plan for each – a plan that illustrates in detail how we will be satisfying the mark scheme's criteria. Please do keep in mind that, when operating under timed conditions, your plans will necessarily be less detailed than those that appear in this volume.

Now, you might be asking whether three or four themes is best. The truth is, you should do whatever you feel most comfortable with: the examiner is looking for an original, creative answer, and not sitting there counting the themes. So if you think you are quick enough to cover four, then great. However, if you would rather do three to make sure you do each theme justice, that's also fine. I sometimes suggest that my student pick four themes, but make the fourth one smaller – sort of like an afterthought, or an observation that turns things on their head. That way, if they feel they won't have time to explore this fourth theme in its own right, they can always give it a quick mention in the conclusion instead.

The view from Calton Hill - again, a spot in Stevenson's native Edinburgh. Stevenson once remarked that 'of all places for a view, this Calton Hill is perhaps the best.'

Before I move forward in earnest, I believe it to be worthwhile to run through the four Assessment Objectives the exam board want you to cover in your response – if only to demonstrate how effective the thematic response can be. I would argue that the first Assessment Objective (AO1) – the one that wants candidates to 'read, understand and respond to texts' and which is worth 12 of the total 34 marks up for grabs – will be wholly satisfied by selecting strong themes, then fleshing them out with quotes. Indeed, when it comes to identifying the top-scoring candidates for AO1, the mark scheme explicitly tells examiners to look for a 'critical, exploratory, conceptualised response' that makes 'judicious use of precise references' – the word 'concept' is a synonym of theme, and 'judicious references' simply refers to quotes that appropriately support the theme you've chosen.

The second Assessment Objective (AO2) – which is also responsible for 12 marks – asks students to 'analyse the language, form and structure used by a writer to create meanings and effects, using relevant subject terminology where appropriate.' As noted, you will already be quoting from the novel as you back up your themes, and it is a natural progression to then analyse the language techniques used. In fact, this is far more effective than simply observing language techniques (personification here, alliteration there), because by discussing how the language techniques relate to and shape the theme, you will also be demonstrating how the writer 'create[s] meanings and effects.'

Now, in my experience, language analysis is the most important element of AO2 – perhaps 8 of the 12 marks will go towards language analysis. You will also notice, however, that AO2 asks students to comment on 'form and structure.' Again, the thematic approach has your back – because though simply jamming in a point on form or structure will feel jarring, when you bring these points up while discussing a theme, as a means to further a thematic argument, you will again organically be discussing the way it 'create[s] meanings and effects.'

AO3 requires you to 'show understanding of the relationships between texts and the contexts in which they were written' and is responsible for a more modest 6 marks in total. These are easy enough to weave into a thematic argument; indeed, the theme gives the student a chance to bring up context in a relevant and fitting way. After all, you don't want it to look like you've just shoehorned a contextual factoid into the mix.

Finally, you have AO4 – known also as "spelling and grammar." Technically speaking, there are no AO4 marks up for grabs in this particular section of the paper. That said, I would still suggest that you take care on this front. The examiners are human beings, and if you are demonstrating a strong grasp of spelling and grammar, most examiners (whether rightly or wrongly!) will still be more inclined to mark your paper more generously.

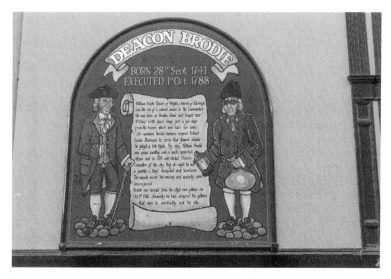

A sign outside Deacon Brodie's Tavern in Edinburgh. Deacon Brodie is frequently acknowledged as an inspiration for Stevenson's novel. Brodie was a respected city councillor in Eighteenth Century Edinburgh; however, it eventually transpired that he was leading a secret life of crime, and he was hung in 1788.

My hope is that this book, by demonstrating how to tease out themes from an extract, will help you feel more confident in doing so yourself. I believe it is also worth mentioning that the themes I have picked out are by no means definitive. Asked the very same question, someone else may pick out different themes, and write an answer that is just as good (if not better!). Obviously the exam is not likely to be fun – my memory of them is pretty much the exact opposite. But still, this is one of the very few chances that you will get at GCSE level to actually be creative. And to my mind at least, that was always more enjoyable – if *enjoyable* is the right word – than simply demonstrating that I had memorised loads of facts.

ESSAY PLAN ONE

READ THE FOLLOWING EXTRACT FROM CHAPTER 1 (STORY OF THE DOOR) OF THE STRANGE CASE OF DR JEKYLL AND MR HYDE AND THEN ANSWER THE QUESTION THAT FOLLOWS.

This extract is the first paragraph of the novel and introduces the reader to Mr Utterson.

Mr Utterson the lawyer was a man of a rugged countenance that was never lighted by a smile; cold, scanty and embarrassed in discourse; backward in sentiment; lean, long, dusty, dreary and yet somehow lovable. At friendly meetings, and when the wine was to his taste, something eminently human beaconed from his eye; something indeed which never found its way into his talk, but which spoke not only in these silent symbols of the after-dinner face, but more often and loudly in the acts of his life. He was austere with himself; drank gin when he was alone, to mortify a taste for vintages; and though he enjoyed the theatre, had not crossed the doors of one for twenty years. But he had an approved tolerance for others; sometimes wondering, almost with envy, at the high pressure of spirits involved in their misdeeds; and in any extremity inclined to help rather than to reprove. "I incline to Cain's heresy," he used to say quaintly: "I let my brother go to the devil in his own way." In this character, it was frequently his fortune to be the last reputable acquaintance and the last good influence in the lives of down-going men. And to such as these, so long as they came about his chambers, he never marked a shade of change in his demeanour.

No doubt the feat was easy to Mr Utterson; for he was undemonstrative at the best, and even his friendship seemed to be founded in a similar catholicity of good-nature. It is the mark of a modest man to accept his friendly circle ready-made from the hands of opportunity; and that was the lawyer's way. His friends were those of his own blood or those whom he had known the longest; his affections, like ivy, were the growth of time, they implied no aptness in the object.

Starting with this extract, explore the extent to which Stevenson presents Utterson as an outsider.

Write about:

• **how Stevenson presents Utterson as an outsider in this extract.**

• **how Stevenson presents Utterson as an outsider in the rest of the novel.**

Introduction

The formula I tend to suggest for writing introductions is as follows: first, offer some (very brief!) historical context, so you are scoring AO3 marks off the bat; next, hint at the themes your essay will be exploring, since this will warm the examiner up to start awarding you AO1 marks (the marks reserved for conceptual understanding).

"Since polite Victorian society was governed by an overwhelming pressure to conform to societal mores, the fear of the outsider – be it the Irish Fenian, or the outlawed homosexual – was all the more pronounced.[1] Stevenson's portrait of a hyper-reserved Utterson demonstrates how the pressure on men to conform to a stoic paradigm paradoxically functioned to detach them from mankind. That said, Utterson's tendency to tangle with more blatant outsiders (not least, Jekyll-cum-Hyde) suggests that he can alternatively be construed as explicitly residing on the peripheries of polite society."[2]

Theme/Paragraph One: In this extract, Utterson is portrayed as lacking (or perhaps reticent to deploy) the ordinary tools of expression that would allow him to communicate with his fellow man, thereby leaving him outside of human discourse.

- As the reader is given a précis of Utterson's personality, what is perhaps most striking is his lack of expressiveness.[3] That the reader is informed in the opening sentence that Utterson's 'countenance...was never lighted by a smile' signals not only Utterson's reticence to engage in non-verbal communication, but also, through the structural choice of opening with this observation, that this reticence is key to understanding his personality: it functions as a kind of epigraph for Utterson the man.[4] [*AO1 for advancing the argument with a judiciously selected quote; AO2 for the close analysis of the language and discussing how structure shapes meaning*].

- Moreover, although the reader is informed that, when drinking, 'something eminently human beaconed from [Utterson's] eye,' what is more interesting is the notion this something 'never found its way into his talk.' Implicit here is the notion that Utterson's words lacked humanity, or could even be construed as *in*human. This redoubles the sense that Utterson's hobbled expressive capabilities place him outside regular human discourse. Tellingly, while he enjoys the theatre – an art-form that embodies expressiveness – he had not visited one in 'twenty years,' and he is explicitly described as 'undemonstrative.' [*AO2 for the close analysis of the language*].

- *Elsewhere in the novel*: The notion that Utterson's muted expressiveness utterly detaches him from mankind is not borne out in the novel: after all, while often solitary, he still socialises with other men (Enfield on walks; Jekyll and Lanyon at dinner) and displays a range of emotions. Indeed, even this extract hints that he is still to be considered somewhat social: it refers to his 'ready-made' friendship 'circle.' In any case, Stevenson seems to be suggesting that if Utterson *is* to be considered an outsider for his repressed ways, then so too should Victorian middle class men *en masse* – all of whom, due to societal pressure to manifest stoicism and decorum, wind up excluded from much of the human experience. [*AO3 for invoking historical context that helps to decode the text*].

Theme/Paragraph Two: While Utterson might be considered an outsider insofar as he embodies Victorian male repression, he might also be considered an outsider for his tendency to seek the company of more blatant outsiders, which in fact puts him at odds with polite society.

- There is an interesting paradox at play in the narrator's observation that Utterson frequently found himself 'the last reputable acquaintance... in the lives of down-going men.' After all, the fact that Utterson chooses to associate with 'down-going men' implicitly threatens to compromise his stated reputability. The phrase 'down-going men' conjures an image of physical descent: a motif that appears persistently in Gothic fiction to connote transgression, and thus functions to emphasise the aberrant behaviour of Utterson's associates.[5] [*AO1 for advancing the argument with a judiciously selected quote; AO2 for the close analysis of the language*].
- *Elsewhere in the novel*: The idea that Utterson's association with outliers might alter his identity is broached when Utterson resolves to investigate Mr Hyde, and tellingly decides that: "If he be Mr Hyde... I shall be Mr Seek." The turn of phrase renders Utterson as a doppelgänger to Hyde – the novel's prime outsider – thereby ensuring that Utterson's identity is defined in relation to Hyde.[6] The use of the

doppelgänger to link the supposedly respectable to the outlier is seen in other Gothic texts: in Mary Shelley's early Nineteenth Century novel, *Frankenstein*, the eponymous doctor's doppelgänger is the monster himself.[7] [*AO1 for advancing the argument with a judiciously selected quote; AO3 for invoking historical-literary context*].

Theme/Paragraph Three: Utterson is characterised as someone who exists beyond the urge to judge and the urge to meddle; though this characterisation is subverted as the novel unfolds.

- Throughout the extract, Utterson is portrayed as existing beyond the desire to judge, or meddle in the business of, others: he is described as having an 'approved tolerance for others,' and as following a *laissez-faire* dictum: 'I let my brother go to the devil in his own way.'[8] As a result, Utterson positions himself as an individual who takes care to remain outside the affairs of others – be it judging those affairs, or seeking to impact upon them. [*AO1 for advancing the argument with a judiciously selected quote*].

- *Elsewhere in the novel*: However, while Utterson may be positioned as an outsider to other people's affairs in this extract, this is thoroughly subverted as the book unfolds. Indeed, the chapter seven sequence in which Utterson and Poole forcefully break into Jekyll's chamber – as Jekyll-cum-Hyde begs him to relent ('Utterson... for God's sake, have mercy!') – symbolically encapsulates Utterson's refusal to remain on the peripheries of other people's affairs. [*AO1 for advancing the argument with a judiciously selected quote*].

Theme/Paragraph Four: Although Utterson is a central presence in the novel – the reader discovers things at the same pace as Utterson – the fact that all passages relating to him are rendered in the third person positions him as an outsider to the reader.

- Although this extract marks Utterson out as a protagonist, the fact it is written in the third person positions him as an outsider to the reader: the reader is not given direct access to his thoughts. The narrative draws attention to this by domiciling a few first-person phrases within this paragraph – "I incline to Cain's heresy" – thus implicitly inviting the reader to consider an alternative narrative mode, one Stevenson eschews, that would *not* have placed Utterson beyond the reader. The density of the text in this extract – there is just a single paragraph break – allows the mise-en-page to mirror Utterson's impenetrability.[9] [*AO1 for advancing the argument with a judiciously selected quote; AO2 for the close analysis of the language and discussing how form shapes meaning*].
- *Elsewhere in the novel*: Furthermore, while the reader experiences things at the same time as Utterson, Utterson is rarely at the centre of the action. Generally, the action has already taken place, and Utterson, detective-like, is piecing it together afterwards. For the duration of the novel's final two chapters ('Lanyon's Narrative;' 'Henry Jekyll's Full

Statement of the Case') Utterson is reading along with the reader, and is locked out of the action.

- It should not go unnoticed that Jekyll-cum-Hyde, the book's more obvious outsider, is given a first person narrative at the end of the novel, and that Utterson is never granted such intimate treatment. In terms of narrative, Utterson is arguably a greater outsider than Jekyll-cum-Hyde. [*AO2* for *discussing how form shapes meaning*].

Conclusion

This has wound up being a meaty, four-themed essay, so I am pretty confident we are adequately satisfying the exam board's AO1 criteria. As a result, I am going to lace my conclusive remarks with literary and historical context, in order to mop up any remaining AO3 marks that may be going spare.

"In Gothic fiction, the monstrous outsider is frequently used as a vehicle to expose the flaws and contradictions of mainstream society; that is, the outsider paradoxically captures the essence of the mainstream. The way Utterson straddles the mainstream and outsider worlds – one 'reputable' and Jekyllian, one 'down-going' and Hydian – hints at the secret symmetry between them. Indeed, the latter is not truly on the outside, but is in fact lurking in the heart of the former. This was true of Victorian London, where, beneath a respectable veneer, prostitution and violence ran rampant."

ESSAY PLAN TWO

I n this extract, an unnamed maid witnesses a murderous encounter between Mr Hyde and Sir Danvers Carew.

And as she so sat she became aware of an aged beautiful gentleman with white hair, drawing near along the lane; and advancing to meet him, another and very small gentleman, to whom at first she paid less attention. When they had come within speech (which was just under the maid's eyes) the older man bowed and accosted the other with a very pretty manner of politeness. It did not seem as if the subject of his address were of great importance; indeed, from his pointing, it sometimes appeared as if he were only inquiring his way; but the moon shone on his face as he spoke, and the girl was pleased to watch it, it seemed to breathe such an innocent and old-world kindness of disposition, yet with something high too, as of a well-founded self-content. Presently her eye wandered to the other, and she was surprised to recognise in him a certain Mr

Hyde, who had once visited her master and for whom she had conceived a dislike. He had in his hand a heavy cane, with which he was trifling; but he answered never a word, and seemed to listen with an ill-contained impatience. And then all of a sudden he broke out in a great flame of anger, stamping with his foot, brandishing the cane, and carrying on (as the maid described it) like a madman. The old gentleman took a step back, with the air of one very much surprised and a trifle hurt; and at that Mr Hyde broke out of all bounds and clubbed him to the earth. And next moment, with ape-like fury, he was trampling his victim under foot and hailing down a storm of blows, under which the bones were audibly shattered and the body jumped upon the roadway. At the horror of these sights and sounds, the maid fainted.

Starting with this extract, explore how Stevenson portrays violence in the novel.

Write about:

• **how Stevenson presents violence in this extract.**

• **how Stevenson presents violence in the rest of the novel.**

Introduction

Once again, I am starting with the one-two punch of historical context, followed by hints at a thematic framework.

"Although many strata in Victorian society sought to project gentility, the frequent incidents of major violence – be it the 1882 Phoenix Park political assassination, or the dynamiting of underground railways in 1883 – threatened to subvert this effort. Stevenson's portrayals of violence (including this sequence involving the assassination of a politician) not only frames violence as a regressive, atavistic activity, but also seeks to present it as a distinctly male pursuit that is often deployed as a spectacle to titillate and entertain."

Theme/Paragraph One: By emphasising Hyde's animalistic and unhinged conduct, violence is presented as a natural means of expression for the regressive and atavistic.

- As the encounter between Danvers and Hyde reaches its violent denouement, the onlooker – the maid at the window – draws attention to Hyde's unhinged and animalistic demeanour. By likening him to 'a madman,' and observing that he was acting 'out of all bounds,' the maid places focus on Hyde's lack of self control, while the invocation of his 'ape-like fury' hints that his violence is indicative of a animalistic precursor in the evolutionary chain – a hint that would have been particularly disturbing to a Victorian audience who, as a result of Darwin's recent works, were hyper aware of *homo-sapiens* closeness to primates. That Hyde is observed to be 'trampling his victim under foot' further cements the link between violence and regressive animalism: he is behaving as though a stampeding animal. [*AO1 for advancing the argument with a judiciously selected quote; AO2 for the close analysis of the language; AO3 for invoking historical/scientific context to decode the text*].

- The sprawling sentence in which the stampeding is detailed uses form to mimic Hyde's out-of-control behaviour. The phrase 'with ape-like fury' is an interpolated clause, a kind of 'out of all bounds' addition, whereas the stacking of verbs – 'trampling;' 'hailing;' 'shattered;' 'jumped' – gives the sentence a momentum that almost threatens to trample the reader. [*AO2 for discussing how form shapes meaning*].

- *Elsewhere in the novel*: Hyde's other key act of violence – namely, his trampling of a child as described by Enfield in the opening chapter – not only uncannily mirrors this scene with its motif of an animalistic stampeding, but also seeks to place explicit emphasis on Hyde's lack of self control: he is described as 'some damned Juggernaut.' [*AO1 for advancing the argument with a judiciously selected quote*].

Theme/Paragraph Two: Violence is portrayed as belonging to the domain of men: it is conducted invariably by men, often while wielding a phallic object.[1] The females of the novel are passive onlookers and victims.

- Central to this extract is the phallic 'heavy cane' Hyde

deploys as a weapon: he is seen as 'brandishing the cane' just as he is about to launch his offensive; he then uses it to club Danvers to death. Seen through a Freudian lens, this club can be construed as a phallus, drawing attention to the distinct maleness of this act of violence.[2] Indeed, the idea that Stevenson perceives violence as a distinctly male activity is underscored by the (very limited) role of women in the novel. This extract relays a female maid's account of the violent encounter, and there is great emphasis on her passivity and alienation from the violence: not only is she a mere onlooker, but she is so disturbed that she 'faint[s].' Moreover, the other key female in the novel – the trampled child of chapter one – is pointedly the victim of male violence. [*AO1 for advancing the argument with a judiciously selected quote*].

- *Elsewhere in the novel*: It ought to be noted that all other non-Hydian violence in the novel is also perpetrated by men; for instance, Utterson's violent entry into Jekyll-cum-Hyde's cabinet in chapter eight, which again involves a phallic weapon: an axe. If one were to take the Freudian reading a step further, it could be argued that the novel's violence is not just perpetrated by men, but should also be understood as *sexual*. Homosexuality was illegal in Victorian England, and thus taboo. Stevenson's dramatisation of violence – often involving phallic objects; in Utterson's case, involving a penetrative act – could be seen as an oblique way of communicating explosive homoerotic passions. [*AO3 for invoking historical context to decode the text*].

Theme/Paragraph Three: Violence is cast as a spectacle – something that is to be consumed by an audience in order to induce an emotional response.

- The maid is also interesting as a spectator. As a result of her geographical positioning (she is watching from above at a window) the maid is cast almost as though an audience member watching from a private box. The extract also places emphasis on her eyes and thus her role of voyeur: the action 'was just under the maid's eyes' – the word 'under' not only delineating a physical location, but also drawing attention to the fact it was under her active observation – and her 'eye wandered' from one character to the other. Stevenson seems to be suggesting that violence in his novel should be treated as a spectacle, perhaps even a form of entertainment and titillation. Indeed, the maid's histrionic response to the violence (she faints, and at the end of the paragraph for structural emphasis) seems to confirm the violence's histrionic nature.[3] [*AO1 for advancing the argument with a judiciously selected quote; AO2 for the close analysis of the language and for discussing how structure shapes meaning*].

- *Elsewhere in the novel:* The use of a window to cast an event as a spectacle is also used when, later in the novel, Enfield and Utterson spot Jekyll in a window. However, the spectacular violence involved in the Jekyll-to-Hyde transformation (for it *is* certainly a form of violence) is tantalisingly removed from view by a curtain, emulating the curtain of a theatre.

- Violence, be it in sports such as boxing or novels, was a common form of entertainment in Victorian England. Indeed, Stevenson's novel as a whole was just such an example: a product in which sequences of violence are deployed to titillate. [*AO3 for invoking historical context to illuminate the text*].

Conclusion

Although we already have a very meaty essay, I have another theme up my sleeve that I'd like to briefly discuss – namely, that Stevenson frames violence as a tool that drives forward the plot. As a result, I am going to integrate it into my conclusion; though, for good measure, I am going to start off with one final nod to historical context (AO3).

"It is little surprise, given the ongoing acts of terrorism in London perpetrated by Irish revolutionaries, that the Victorian clergyman, Charles Kingley, described the Irish as 'white chimpanzees:' animalism was bound up with violence in the Nineteenth Century imagination. Yet violence in Stevenson's novels functions in a number of ways. Indeed, perhaps the most important way Stevenson portrays violence is as a narrative driver: the trampling of the girl entangles Utterson in events; the murder of Danvers renders Hyde an untenable guise for Jekyll; and Utterson's storming of the cabinet precipitates Jekyll-cum-Hyde's suicide. Stevenson portrays violence as the crucial engine of the plot, whose 'storm of blows' keep the narrative from stalling."

This engraving of the Thames from 1868 depicts a patrol boat (in the foreground), seeking to protect a floating cargo boat full of gunpowder (back left) from Irish Fenian terrorists.

ESSAY PLAN THREE

READ THE FOLLOWING EXTRACT FROM CHAPTER 7 (INCIDENT AT THE WINDOW) OF THE STRANGE CASE OF DR JEKYLL AND MR HYDE AND THEN ANSWER THE QUESTION THAT FOLLOWS.

At this point in the novel, Utterson and Enfield, while out for a walk, spot Jekyll sitting within his home.

The court was very cool and a little damp, and full of premature twilight, although the sky, high up overhead, was still bright with sunset. The middle one of the three windows was half-way open; and sitting close beside it, taking the air with an infinite sadness of mien, like some disconsolate prisoner, Utterson saw Dr Jekyll.

"What! Jekyll!" he cried. "I trust you are better."

"I am very low, Utterson," replied the doctor, drearily, "very low. It will not last long, thank God."

"You stay too much indoors," said the lawyer. "You should be out, whipping up the circulation like Mr Enfield and me. (This is my cousin— Mr Enfield— Dr Jekyll.) Come, now; get your hat and take a quick turn with us."

"You are very good," sighed the other. "I should like to very much; but no, no, no, it is quite impossible; I dare not. But indeed, Utterson, I am very glad to see you; this is really a great pleasure; I would ask you and Mr Enfield up, but the place is really not fit."

"Why then," said the lawyer, good-naturedly, "the best thing we can do is to stay down here and speak with you from where we are."

"That is just what I was about to venture to propose," returned the doctor with a smile. But the words were hardly uttered, before the smile was struck out of his face and succeeded by an expression of such abject terror and despair, as froze the very blood of the two gentlemen below. They saw it but for a glimpse, for the window was instantly thrust down; but that glimpse had been sufficient, and they turned and left the court without a word. In silence, too, they traversed the by-street; and it was not until they had come into a neighbouring thorough-fare, where even upon a Sunday there were still some stirrings of life, that Mr Utterson at last turned and looked at his companion. They were both pale; and there was an answering horror in their eyes.

Starting with this extract, how does Stevenson present Dr Jekyll as possessing a troubled mind?

Write about:

• **how Stevenson presents Dr Jekyll in this extract.**

• **how Stevenson presents Dr Jekyll as a troubled character in the novel as a whole.**

Introduction

"Given that the late Nineteenth Century saw unprecedented interest in parsing the inner-workings of the human mind – indeed, it was when Sigmund Freud, the father of psychoanalysis, came to prominence – it is little surprise this interest appeared in fiction of the era. Jekyll's thralled and troubled mindset here is revealed not only through his fatalistic words, but also through the symbolism of the physical landscape, and the contagiousness of the despair he exudes."

Theme/Paragraph One: Jekyll's mental strife is echoed in both the prison-like geography of the court and the twilight, both of which point to his psychological entrapment.

- It is striking that, before Jekyll's presence is noted, the narrator takes pains to describe the physical environs. The narrator observes that the action is unfolding in a 'court,' a physical space that evokes enclosure, and its inhospitality is communicated in no uncertain terms:

the conditions are austere ('very cool and a little damp') and the 'twilight' hints at the imminence of night's oppressive darkness. The claustrophobia is also heightened by the tableau of three windows, with Jekyll appearing in 'the middle of the three:' Jekyll is visually entrapped between two windows, echoing his mental thrall. Indeed, Stevenson ensures the reader views the environs through the lens of entrapment with a simile likening Jekyll to 'some disconsolate prisoner.' [*AO1 for advancing the argument with a judiciously selected quote; AO2 for the close analysis of the language*].

- One might note that by setting the action in a 'court,' and having a lawyer present (Utterson is described as 'the lawyer' in this extract), Stevenson cleverly invites the reader to also consider a court of law – a location where criminals are handed down jail sentences. [*AO2 for the close analysis of the language*].

- *Elsewhere in the novel*: The physical environment is used time and again to convey Jekyll-cum-Hyde's thralled mental state: for instance, shortly after this sequence, Jekyll-cum-Hyde is holed up in a cabinet in his theatre, a prison within a prison. The idea that physical space could reflect a mental state would have been cemented in the Victorian consciousness by the increasing prominence of insane asylums – physical spaces that explicitly sought to categorise its occupants' mental state. Edgar Allan Poe's 1852 short story – whose title, 'The System of Doctor Tarr and Professor Fether,' is almost a doppelganger of Stevenson's – features just such an asylum. [*AO3 for invoking historical-literary context to illuminate the text*].

Theme/Paragraph Two: Jekyll's troubled mindset is expressed explicitly through his words and his manner of speech, all of which point to fatalism, depression, and a terminal lack of resolve.

- Jekyll's dialogue in this extract does not seek to cloak his troubled mental state: he concedes explicitly that he is feeling 'very low' – the refrain of the phrase not only hammering home his depression, but also invoking the Gothic motif of descent as a means to reflect the intensity of his depression. His observation that 'it will not last long, thank God,' does not hint at redemption; it smacks of a fatalistic understanding that his end is nigh. One might also note that, as he reacts to Utterson's social invitation, Jekyll's response seems to embody irresolution and rudderlessness. For one thing, the central conceit is Jekyll second-guessing himself: his initial 'I should like to' transmuting into a stuttering 'no, no, no.' For another, the way in which these two snaking sentences are elongated with a litany of semi-colons uses form to allow the sentences themselves to reflect Jekyll's uncertain and inconclusive mindset. [*AO1 for advancing the argument with a judiciously selected quote; AO2 for the close analysis of the language and for discussing how form shapes meaning*].
- If Jekyll's words were not explicit enough, the way the narrator describes his manner drives his fatalism and depression home: Jekyll is described as sighing ('sighed the other') and he speaks 'drearily.' [*AO2 for the close analysis of the language*].
- *Elsewhere in the novel*: Early in the novel, while

Stevenson has Jekyll conceal the truth, he still has his manner and language reveal his troubled mindset: for instance, in the second chapter, when Utterson asks him about Hyde, Jekyll is described as 'pale to the very lips.' It is interesting that this novel (unlike such Gothic fiction as Stoker's *Dracula* (1897), in which the eponymous monster is never heard from) gives a whole first-person chapter to Jekyll-cum-Hyde – that is, the monster himself. Stevenson is allowing language to give a direct insight into Jekyll-cum-Hyde's troubled mind. [*AO1 for advancing the argument with a judiciously selected quote; AO3 for invoking literary context to illuminate the text*].

Theme/Paragraph Three: Utterson and Enfield at first highlight Jekyll's troubled mind through their juxtaposing merriment. At the close of the passage, their troubled mindset is a reflection of Jekyll's own: his mental disarray is contagious.

- Jekyll's troubled mindset is thrown into sharper relief by the high spirits exhibited by Utterson and Enfield: whereas Utterson talks 'good-naturedly' warmly invites Jekyll to join them ('get your hat and take a quick turn with us'), Jekyll goes from downbeat to profoundly disturbed: 'an expression of such abject terror and despair.' If the expression of 'terror and despair' itself was not enough to convey Jekyll's tumultuous mindset, its stark contrast to Utterson and Enfield's calm ensures the reader grasps the message. [*AO1 for advancing the argument with a judiciously selected quote*]

- However, what is perhaps even more effective at conveying Jekyll's troubled mindset is the way in which its toxicity seems to colonise Utterson and Enfield's mental states, too. As they digest Jekyll's expression, the narrator observes how it 'froze [their] very blood.' The extract closes with the observation that both men were 'pale' and sporting 'an answering horror in their eyes.' Jekyll's troubled mindset has proved so potent that it has in fact shown itself to be contagious, creating an 'answering horror' in those who encounter it. [*AO2 for the close analysis of the language*].

- *Elsewhere in the novel*: It might be noted that Jekyll's alter-ego, Hyde, also has his tumultuous (and indeed murderous) internal state reflected – and thus further revealed – in those who encounter him. In the opening chapter, Enfield observes how Hyde inspired in those who accosted him a "desire to kill him.'

Conclusion

I do have a final point I want to cover in the conclusion: the idea that Hyde himself is the most powerful technique Stevenson employs to reveal the state of Jekyll's mind. I'm hoping this will score some final AO1 marks as I tie things up...

"Perhaps the most important technique Stevenson uses to convey Jekyll's troubled soul has flown under the radar: namely, the very existence of Hyde. After all, as Jekyll here pulls back the curtain at the apotheosis of his distress (a motion emulating a theatrical curtain falling at a cliff-hanger), the reader in retrospect understands that Hyde is clambering out of Jekyll. However, while deploying the doppelgänger of Hyde is the most effective way to express Jekyll's mindset, it should be noted that, by having Utterson and Enfield mirror his distress, Stevenson is subtly casting them as temporary doppelgängers, revealing Jekyll's mindset in Hyde's absence."

ESSAY PLAN FOUR

READ THE FOLLOWING EXTRACT FROM
CHAPTER 8 (THE LAST NIGHT) OF THE
STRANGE CASE OF DR JEKYLL AND MR
HYDE AND THEN ANSWER THE QUESTION
THAT FOLLOWS.

In this extract, Poole has arrived at Utterson's home after suspecting there to be an intruder within his master's home.

Mr Utterson was sitting by his fireside one evening after dinner, when he was surprised to receive a visit from Poole.

"Bless me, Poole, what brings you here?" he cried; and then taking a second look at him, "What ails you?" he added; "is the doctor ill?"

"Mr Utterson," said the man, "there is something wrong."

"Take a seat, and here is a glass of wine for you," said the lawyer. "Now, take your time, and tell me plainly what you want."

"You know the doctor's ways, sir," replied Poole, "and how he shuts himself up. Well, he's shut up again in the cabinet; and I don't like it, sir—I wish I may die if I like it. Mr Utterson, sir, I'm afraid."

"Now, my good man," said the lawyer, "be explicit. What are you afraid of?"

"I've been afraid for about a week," returned Poole, doggedly disregarding the question, "and I can bear it no more."

The man's appearance amply bore out his words; his manner was altered for the worse; and except for the moment when he had first announced his terror, he had not once looked the lawyer in the face. Even now, he sat with the glass of wine untasted on his knee, and his eyes directed to a corner of the floor. "I can bear it no more," he repeated.

"Come," said the lawyer, "I see you have some good reason, Poole; I see there is something seriously amiss. Try to tell me what it is."

"I think there's been foul play," said Poole, hoarsely.

"Foul play!" cried the lawyer, a good deal frightened and rather inclined to be irritated in consequence. "What foul play! What does the man mean?"

"I daren't say, sir," was the answer; "but will you come along with me and see for yourself?"

Starting with this extract, explore how Stevenson generates mystery and tension in The *Strange Case of Dr Jekyll and Mr Hyde*.

Write about:

- **how Stevenson creates mystery and tension in this extract.**

- **how Stevenson creates mystery and tension in the novel as a whole.**

Introduction

This time, I am going to integrate some literary context into the introduction – which will also be scoring us early AO3 marks.

"A hallmark of the Gothic genre – which was popularised in the Eighteenth Century, and remained a force throughout the Nineteenth – was the intentional cultivation of tension and mystery: indeed, Horace Walpole, the author of the first Gothic novel, claimed he had discovered his manuscript in order to generate mystery.[1] Stevenson's novel, as shown in this extract, also uses the withholding of information to generate mystery; however, it deploys other powerful techniques – including depictions of physical distress, and juxtapositions – to ramp up tension."

Theme/Paragraph One: This extract sees Poole persistently withhold information from both the reader and Utterson, a technique that is used in different manifestations throughout the novel to create mystery.

- Although at many points, Utterson directly asks Poole the reason for his visit – 'tell me plainly;' 'be explicit;' 'What foul play?'– Poole, on each occasion, refuses to divulge. The closest he comes to an answer is the suggestion his 'master' is 'shut up again in the cabinet,' which again declines to get to the crux of his suspicions: that an interloper has taken Jekyll's place. The form deployed in Poole's answers further contributes to a sense of evasion: for instance, the use of a dash in the exclamation ('I don't like it, sir—I wish I may die if I like it') creates a hard pause that draws attention to the essential emptiness of his answer. [*AO1 for advancing the argument with a judiciously selected quote; AO2 for the close analysis of the language and for discussing how form shapes meaning*].

- The withholding of information is powerfully used here to create mystery. Indeed, that the subject under discussion is a locked room (a recurring motif in Gothic fiction) is particularly fitting: the reader is being locked out of information.

- <u>*Elsewhere in the novel*</u>: Throughout the novel, Stevenson employs withholding tactics: the reader must wait until the final two chapters to learn the mysteries contained in Lanyon and Jekyll's narrative. Moreover, there are a number of mysteries that are never resolved. For one thing, the reader never learns much about the nature of Hyde's illicit activities. For another, it is unclear whether Hyde had a hand in authoring the final chapter: after all, the letter Hyde sends to Lanyon is written in Jekyll's voice. Perhaps this tactic is fitting for a Victorian novel, given that the era was characterised by the persistent repression of emotions and feelings. [*AO3 for placing the text in historical context*].

Theme/Paragraph Two: The physical depiction of the unsettled Poole in this extract functions to create tension – not least because some of his mannerisms seem almost to echo Hyde's.

- Stevenson in this extract takes pains to communicate Poole's state of distress. Not only do Poole and Utterson's comments make his disarray clear – Utterson tellingly expresses concern ('what ails you?') before Poole speaks, and Poole openly concedes he has 'been afraid for about a week' – but so too does Poole's stilted verbal patter: his stuttering repetition of 'sir;' the way he repeats the phrase, 'I can bear it no more.' [*AO2 for the close analysis of the language*].

- However, perhaps most striking is the narrator's depiction of Poole's state: after observing that his 'manner was altered for the worse,' it observes that he persistently avoids making eye contact with Utterson: 'he had not once looked the lawyer in the face.' Aside from being itself a sign of anxiety, it is also a mannerism that is in fact exhibited by Hyde: for instance, when Utterson accosts Hyde in chapter two, it is noted in near identical language that Hyde 'did not look the lawyer in the face.' Not only is there tension in the sheer fact of Poole's distress, but the ante is upped by the notion that Hyde's mannerisms have somehow colonised other individuals. It also hints at the issue at stake: that Hyde has colonised

Jekyll's home. [*AO1 for advancing the argument with judiciously selected quotes*].

- *Elsewhere in the novel*: It ought to be noted that tense depictions of distress induced by Hyde punctuate the novel – chief among them the depiction of Lanyon's shock at witnessing Hyde transform. The shock is so profound that it in fact precipitates Lanyon's death.

Theme/Paragraph Three: Utterson's relative calm, as well as the calm conjured by the setting, juxtaposes with Poole's unsettled demeanour and thus functions to further heighten the tension conjured by Poole's disarray.

- Whereas Poole's demeanour is unsettled, the domestic scene evoked in the initial sentence of this extract places emphasis on calm and creature comforts: Utterson is 'sitting by his fireside' – the 'sitting' implying ease and the fireside invoking security – and Utterson is sated: it is 'after dinner.' Moreover, by establishing this calm domestic space at the extract's opening, Stevenson uses structure to underscore the air of tranquillity. [*AO1 for advancing the argument with a judiciously selected quote; AO2 for the close analysis of the language and discussing how structure shapes meaning*].

- As Poole enters this tranquil space, there is a persistent clash between Poole's anxiety and Utterson's repeated attempts to reinstate calm: he invites Poole to sit – 'take a seat' – and presses him to have some wine ('here's a glass of wine for you'), a luxury good that acts as yet another symbol of comfort and relaxation. The contrast between Utterson's desire to maintain calm and Poole as an engine of angst and tension is emphasised by the quick-fire dialogue, and the litany of competing short paragraph it creates, causing the mise-en-page to reflect this clash of moods. [*AO1 for advancing the argument with judiciously selected quotes; AO2 for discussing how form shapes meaning*].

* *Elsewhere in the novel*: Stevenson's novel as a whole relies on contrasts to create tension and terror; after all, Hyde is horrifying only insofar as he contrasts to Jekyll and the wider codes of conduct demanded by society. A more local example of this might be the incident in which Enfield and Utterson see Jekyll in the window: the two walkers' calm serves to accentuate the tension created by Jekyll's distress.

Conclusion

In this conclusion, I not only lay down a litany of relevant historical observations, but I also link them to one final conceptual observation – that uncertainty is the most important means by which Stevenson generates tension and mystery.

"Stevenson's Britain was shot-through with a pervasive air of uncertainty: economic uncertainty, following an economic depression in the 1870s; nationalistic uncertainty, as a result of the rise of America and Germany; domestic uncertainty, due to Irish and anarchistic terrorism. While Stevenson employs many tactics to conjure mystery and tension, it is ultimately the sowing of uncertainty (the refusal to 'be explicit,' as Utterson puts it) on which he most relies. One need look no further than the tension conjured by the uncertainty of when Jekyll might experience an involuntarily transformation, or the mystery conjured by the uncertainty of what 'impurity' it was that gave Jekyll's potion its transformative powers."

A plaque commemorating Robert Louis Stevenson in Edinburgh. Although *Dr Jekyll and Mr Hyde* is set in London, the writer G. K. Chesteron has argued that throughout the novel the city frequently feels aesthetically reminiscent of Edinburgh.

ESSAY PLAN FIVE

READ THE FOLLOWING EXTRACT FROM
CHAPTER 8 (THE LAST NIGHT) OF THE
STRANGE CASE OF DR JEKYLL AND MR
HYDE AND THEN ANSWER THE QUESTION
THAT FOLLOWS.

A t this point in the novel, **Utterson has just
arrived at Jekyll's home. He has been led
there by Poole, who wants Utterson to help investigate whether an intruder is on the premises.**

The hall, when they entered it, was brightly lighted up; the fire
was built high; and about the hearth the whole of the servants,
men and women, stood huddled together like a flock of sheep.
At the sight of Mr Utterson, the housemaid broke into hysterical whimpering; and the cook, crying out "Bless God! it's Mr
Utterson," ran forward as if to take him in her arms.

"What, what? Are you all here?" said the lawyer peevishly.
"Very irregular, very unseemly; your master would be far from
pleased."

"They're all afraid," said Poole.

Blank silence followed, no one protesting; only the maid lifted her voice and now wept loudly.

"Hold your tongue!" Poole said to her, with a ferocity of accent that testified to his own jangled nerves; and indeed, when the girl had so suddenly raised the note of her lamentation, they had all started and turned towards the inner door with faces of dreadful expectation. "And now," continued the butler, addressing the knife-boy, "reach me a candle, and we'll get this through hands at once." And then he begged Mr Utterson to follow him, and led the way to the back garden.

"Now, sir," said he, "you come as gently as you can. I want you to hear, and I don't want you to be heard. And see here, sir, if by any chance he was to ask you in, don't go."

Mr Utterson's nerves, at this unlooked-for termination, gave a jerk that nearly threw him from his balance; but he recollected his courage and followed the butler into the laboratory building through the surgical theatre, with its lumber of crates and bottles, to the foot of the stair. Here Poole motioned him to stand on one side and listen; while he himself, setting down the candle and making a great and obvious call on his resolution, mounted the steps and knocked with a somewhat uncertain hand on the red baize of the cabinet door.

Starting with this extract, explore how Stevenson presents fear in *The Strange Case of Dr Jekyll and Mr Hyde*.

Write about:

• **how Stevenson presents fear in this extract.**

- **how Stevenson presents fear in the novel as a whole.**

Introduction

Notice how I once again invoke political violence as my historical context – just as I did in the earlier essay about portrayals of violence. This shows that you can intelligently manipulate historical and contextual knowledge to the question at hand.

"Given that late Nineteenth Century London was plagued by a string of terrorist attacks (the bombing of Victoria Station in 1884; the attack on Scotland Yard shortly after), it was little surprise a fascination with fear and terror manifested in the era's artistic output.[1] This extract, focusing on individuals who had come into proximity with Hyde, seeks to explore not only the various responses fear induces – the lack of agency it instils in some; the resolve it inspires in others – but also how Stevenson presents it as something that can be inspired through certain artistic techniques."

Theme/Paragraph One: In this extract, fear is presented as robbing individuals of their autonomy, and therefore rendering them dependent on the guidance of others.

- As Utterson enters Jekyll's household, both Utterson and the reader are presented with a tableau of fearful domestic staff – 'the whole of the servants, men and women' – huddled around the fireplace; and that fear is their animating principle is made explicit through Poole's observation: 'They're all afraid.' However, what is most interesting is the simile Stevenson deploys: the staff are 'like a flock of sheep.' Sheep are creatures idiomatically known for their lack of autonomy: instead, they function as a herd, and depend on external guidance. The implication is that fear has sapped the staff of their autonomy, and even their individuality. [*AO1 for advancing the argument with judiciously selected quotes; AO2 for the close analysis of the language*].

- This implication is borne out throughout the passage: the staff are indeed utterly guided by Utterson and Poole; and the subjugation of their individuality to the herd is confirmed by the fact that not one of them is assigned a name (they are merely 'the maid,' 'the knife boy') and that no precise number is given for their ranks. Moreover, the sense of animalistic regression is accentuated by the housemaid's 'hysterical whimpering' – a sound reminiscent of cornered prey. The Victorian audience, with Darwin's research concerning humans' evolution from animals fresh in their minds, would have found this animalistic imagery particularly powerful and disturbing. [*AO2 for the close analysis of the language; AO3 for providing historical-scientific context that illuminates the text*].

- *Elsewhere in the novel*: If in this extract fear reduces individuals to rudderless ciphers, it has an even more profound impact on Lanyon in the aftermath of witnessing Hyde's transformation. Fear does not simply rob him of his autonomy; it robs him of his life

– it proves quite literally (as Lanyon describes it) 'the deadliest terror' and precipitates his death. [*AO1 for advancing the argument with a judiciously selected quote*].

Theme/Paragraph Two: While fear functions to sap some individuals of their autonomy, it is also presented as a force that can galvanise others and endow them with a sense of leadership.

- Whereas the domestic staff in this extract are presented as sheep-like in the face of Hyde-inspired terror, Poole on the other hand seems to channel his evident fear ('jangled nerves') into initiative and action: not only was he the one who sought out Utterson, but he also calls the shots throughout this extract. He tells the maid to 'Hold [her] tongue,' he gives instructions to the knife-boy ('addressing the knife-boy') and Utterson ('I want you to hear I don't want you to be heard'), and he leads Utterson to the source of danger. [*AO1 for advancing the argument with a judiciously selected quote*].

- Utterson, too, appears to be galvanised as opposed to cowed by the Hyde-induced fear: although his 'nerves...gave a jerk that nearly threw him from his balance,' he is able to 'recollect... his courage' and continue with his mission. That the passage ends with Utterson solitarily mounting the stairs, while 'making a great and obvious call on his resolution,' gives structural emphasis to his ability to channel his fear into action. [*AO1 for advancing the argument with a*

*judiciously selected quote; AO2 for discussing how
structure shapes meaning*].

- *Elsewhere in the novel*: Throughout the novel,
  Utterson's fear that Hyde might be exploiting Jekyll
  causes him to take the initiative to investigate the
  situation. When he first sees Hyde, he is struck with
  fear, but this only galvanises him further.

**Theme/Paragraph Three: Throughout this
extract, Utterson treats fear as an emotion of
which one should be ashamed: Mr Utterson is
highly critical of the way in which the staff so
openly display their fear.**

- Utterson's knee-jerk reaction to the domestics' open
  display of fear is one of criticism: he 'peevishly'
  describes it as 'very irregular, very unseemly,' and
  hammers his disapproval home with a one-two punch
  of rhetorical questions: 'What, what? Are you all
  here?' Poole's demand that the maid 'hold [her]
  tongue' seems to indicate that he has internalised
  Utterson's disapproval of exhibitions of strong
  emotions. [*AO1 for advancing the argument with a
  judiciously selected quote; AO2 for the close analysis
  of the language*].
- Ironically enough, as already mentioned, Utterson
  himself is not untouched by fear as he enters this
  tense scenario (his 'nerves...took a jerk'). However,
  instead of externalising fear, he attempts to control
  and conceal these emotions he considers shameful.
  Indeed, while it has been argued that Utterson's
  decision to continue investigating Jekyll's surgery can

be construed as an example of initiative, it could equally be understood as a means of cloaking and concealing his shameful fear. This attitude towards fear must be understood through a prism of Victorian stoicism: men in Stevenson's Britain were expected to repress strong emotions, and, as the Victorian poet Rudyard Kipling put it, 'meet with Triumph and Disaster and treat those two impostors as just the same.' [*AO3 for insightfully placing the text in its historical and literary context*].

- *Elsewhere in the novel*: At the start of Jekyll's narrative, Jekyll states how, as a result of his 'imperious desire to hold his head high,' he concealed his desires and emotions 'with an almost morbid sense of shame,' and it was this shame that motivated his desire to unleash Hyde. This points at the Victorian urge to conceal all strong emotions – not simply fear. [*AO1 for advancing the argument with a judiciously selected quote*].

Theme/Paragraph Four: Aside from looking at the impact of fear, this extract implicitly demonstrates how Stevenson presents fear as an emotion that can be inspired using specific Gothic motifs and linguistic techniques.

- Stevenson, by deploying a range of Gothic tropes, presents fear as an emotion that can be elicited using specific techniques. The darkness in the garden, which is hinted at by the fact Poole and Utterson require a candle, creates a tense and fearful mood. Moreover, the maid's hysterical state is another

Gothic trope that raises the tension: this is reminiscent not only of the sequence (at the denouement of Danvers's murder) when the maid fainted, but also of such Gothic novels as Horace Walpole's *The Castle of Otranto* or Percy Shelley's *Zastrozzi*, in which fainting women were used as shorthand to indicate a fearful situation. [*AO3 for insightfully placing the text in its historical and literary context*].

- Stevenson also endows the dialogue in this extract with a staccato rhythm: a use of form to both indicate the presence of, and to evoke, fear. Aside from the obvious repetitions, you also have more subtle turns of phrases to create this staccato effect: for instance, the half-rhyme on 'hear' and heard' in Poole's comment: 'I want you to hear, and I don't want you to be heard.' This creates a sense of jarring, unsatisfying repetition that induces disquiet in the reader, while also, through the words' aural closeness to Hyde, reminding the reader of the dangers that await.[2] [*AO2 for the close analysis of the language and for discussing how form shapes meaning*].

Conclusion

"In works of the Romantic movement, the sister genre and forerunner to Victorian Gothic, poets meditated at length on the sublime: those forces that transcend and overwhelm. For the domestics in this passage and Lanyon, fear is presented as just such a force. Yet whereas the Romantics embraced expressing emotional extremes, Stevenson (through his stoic mouthpiece,

Utterson) intermingles an acknowledgement of fear's power with a sense of shame towards the emotions it elicits. Moreover, by laying bare the processes by which fear is evoked in the reader, Stevenson in some ways demystifies it, presenting it as the product of an artist's sleight of hand."

ESSAY PLAN SIX

At this point in the novel, Hyde has arrived at Lanyon's house in order to imbibe the potion that will transform him back to Jekyll.

This person (who had thus, from the first moment of his entrance, struck in me what I can only describe as a disgustful curiosity) was dressed in a fashion that would have made an ordinary person laughable; his clothes, that is to say, although they were of rich and sober fabric, were enormously too large for him in every measurement—the trousers hanging on his legs and rolled up to keep them from the ground, the waist of the coat below his haunches, and the collar sprawling wide upon his shoulders. Strange to relate, this ludicrous accoutrement was far from moving me to laughter. Rather, as there was something abnormal and misbegotten in the very essence of the creature that now faced me—something seizing, surprising and revolting—this fresh disparity seemed but to fit in with and to reinforce it; so that to my interest in the man's nature and character, there was added a curiosity as to his origin, his life, his fortune and status in the world.

These observations, though they have taken so great a space to be set down in, were yet the work of a few seconds. My visitor was, indeed, on fire with sombre excitement.

"Have you got it?" he cried. "Have you got it?" And so lively was his impatience that he even laid his hand upon my arm and sought to shake me.

I put him back, conscious at his touch of a certain icy pang along my blood. "Come, sir," said I. "You forget that I have not yet the pleasure of your acquaintance. Be seated, if you please." And I showed him an example, and sat down myself in my customary seat and with as fair an imitation of my ordinary manner to a patient, as the lateness of the hour, the nature of my preoccupations, and the horror I had of my visitor, would suffer me to muster.

Starting with this extract, explore how Stevenson presents evil through Hyde.

Write about:

• how Stevenson presents Mr Hyde and evil in this extract.

• how Stevenson presents Mr Hyde and evil in the novel as a whole.

Introduction

"As the self-regardingly rational forces of the Victorian era sought to categorise and quantify the world, criminality and evil unsurprisingly came under their gaze: for example, the (now debunked) work of Cesare Lombroso, positing a correlation between head shape and criminality, gained particular currency. In this passage, Stevenson also attempts to get the measure of evil, delving into the insatiability Hyde embodies, his absurdities, and his sheer unnaturalness; however, Stevenson ultimately seems to hint that evil is a concept beyond quantification."

Theme/Paragraph One: In this extract, Hyde – and, by extension, evil – is presented as an impatient and insatiable force; however, the extract also hints that evil can induce insatiability in others, and that an insatiable appetite can beget further evil.

- In this extract, Hyde's appetites appear to be both ravenous and insatiable. His demeanour, and his extreme desire to obtain the item he is seeking (the potion), are both testament to this ravenousness: Lanyon describes Hyde as 'on fire with sombre excitement' and is struck by his 'lively impatience,' whereas Hyde twice repeats the phrase: 'Have you got it?' Moreover, the way Hyde 'sought to shake' Lanyon seems to physically manifest his impatience: Hyde is seeking to galvanise Lanyon by shaking him. [*AO1 for advancing the argument with judiciously selected quotes; AO2 for the close analysis of the language*].

- However, what is perhaps most interesting here is the fact that evil can also induce an insatiability which in turn brings about further evil. Lanyon in this extract appears unable to resist knowing more about Hyde: he admits that Hyde induces a 'disgustful curiosity' in him, and concedes that not only did he have an 'interest in the man's nature and character' but also a 'curiosity as to his origin, his life, his fortune, and status.' Sure enough, this insatiable curiosity leads to Lanyon witnessing the lethal sight of Hyde's transformation – indeed, one might observe that the very fact a man found himself enduring such a sight is a kind of instance of evil. [*AO1 for advancing the argument with judiciously selected quotes*].

- Elsewhere in the novel: Arguably, Lanyon's experience here has parallels with Jekyll's journey. Jekyll, too, is possessed with an insatiable curiosity – a scientific one – which led him to unlock the evil of Hyde. This is reminiscent of Mary Shelley's earlier Gothic novel, *Frankenstein*, in which the eponymous protagonist's insatiable curiosity leads to the creation of his monster. [*AO3 for providing historical-literary context that illuminates the text*].

Theme / Paragraph Two: Evil, through the entity as Hyde, is presented as something almost comical and absurd.

- Hyde, curiously, is also portrayed as an entity that is almost comical in his appearance – an effect that is chiefly achieved by the juxtaposition between his diminutive stature and his clothes, which 'were enormously too large for him in every measurement.'

The way Stevenson places a clause in parenthesis within the sprawling first sentence has the form reflect this absurd image: the smaller interpolated clause is cloaked in the larger sentence. That the image Hyde strikes is to be taken as comically absurd is made explicit by Layon's remark that he was 'dressed in a fashion that would have made an ordinary person laughable,' [*AO1 for advancing the argument with judiciously selected quotes; AO2 for discussing how form shapes meaning*].

- Excess is often considered a hallmark of the Gothic genre. However, in this instance, the excess in this visual image seems to at least in part to subvert the seriousness of the evil supposedly embodied in Hyde, almost threatening to render him – and thus evil – a figure of fun.

- *Elsewhere in the novel*: The notion that Hyde in this get-up should be construed as comical is reaffirmed in the following chapter, in which Jekyll-cum-Hyde narrates the same incident, noting how it was 'comical,' and how the cab driver 'could not conceal his mirth.' Stevenson is taking pains to communicate the physical comedy at play. [*AO1 for advancing the argument with judiciously selected quotes*].

Theme/ Paragraph Three: However, while Hyde is presented as almost comically absurd, this is held in uneasy tension with a competing portrayal: Hyde as a figure of transcendental repulsiveness and singular unnaturalness.

- Looking again at Lanyon's comment that Hyde's

clothes 'would have made an ordinary person laughable,' one can see that there is in fact a caveat encoded in the observation: the presence of Hyde himself threatens to undermine the image's comic impetus. If this caveat was not clear enough, Lanyon then makes the point explicit: he observes that the 'ludicrous accoutrement was far from moving me to laughter,' and diagnoses the reason: the 'abnormal and misbegotten' man within the clothes is so aesthetically disturbing that all comic potential is sapped from the image. [*AO1 for advancing the argument with judiciously selected quotes; AO2 for the close analysis of the language*].

- The diction used to describe Hyde's hideousness – he is not only 'abnormal and misbegotten,' but also 'seizing, surprising and revolting' – seem to combine to relay a sense of transcendent repulsiveness. The word 'seizing' is particularly effective, for it seems to both apply to Hyde's staccato mannerisms, but also the shudder-inducing impact he has on others, whereas 'surprising' suggests that his aesthetic falls well outside the bounds of what one might ordinarily encounter. As a result, insofar as Hyde is to be considered as a shorthand for evil, evil seems to be presented as an aesthetic that both surprises and appals, and that seems to manifest a cross between Lombroso's archetypal criminal and a regressed version of humanity – the sort of primate from which Darwin had shown *homo sapiens* to have descended. [*AO1 for advancing the argument with judiciously selected quotes; AO2 for the close analysis of the language; AO3 for providing insightful historical-scientific context*].

- *Elsewhere in the novel*: The portrayal of Hyde as aesthetically repulsive is persistent throughout the novel. Enfield's initial description of Hyde in the opening chapter is a case in point: he recalls Hyde giving him a look 'so ugly that it brought out the sweat on me like running.'

Theme/Paragraph Four: The contradiction between Hyde's comic and repulsive aesthetics are not an error, so much as it is the very essence of Hyde, and thus evil. Evil is something that defies categorisation.

- Near the end of the extract, after inviting Hyde to 'be seated,' Lanyon adopts 'as fair an imitation of [his] ordinary manner to a patient.' This hints that Lanyon is attempting to take an empirical approach to Hyde: trying, in a doctoral fashion, to diagnose *what* he is. However, Lanyon is doomed to fail, since Hyde – and the evil he embodies – is characterised by his existence beyond categorisation. [*AO1 for advancing the argument with judiciously selected quotes; AO2 for the close analysis of the language*].
- The aforementioned paradox – that Hyde is both comical, yet entirely unfunny and horrifying – hints at how Stevenson construes evil. Evil in this novel is paradoxical and defies categorisation. It is both larger than life, and something that can be contained within Hyde's body. It is something comical and ridiculous, but also something unsettling and aesthetically offensive. It is something totally inhuman, yet at the same time, something that every human has lingering

inside them. One might note that Hyde is not even definitively evil; rather, he defies such easy categorisation by carrying with him at all times a vestige of Jekyll, who yearns to revert to a Jekyllian state.

- *Elsewhere in the novel*: The novel's narrative structure – a hodgepodge of different narratives, cobbled together non-chronologically – itself defies categorisation, thereby mirroring the way Hyde and evil are portrayed in the novel. [*AO2 for discussing how structure shapes meaning*].

Conclusion

"The chapter proceeding this extract is labelled 'Henry Jekyll's Full Statement of the Case.' Yet this categorisation again falls short, as the reader is left uncertain whether Hyde had a hand in its composition; after all, Hyde sends Lanyon a letter mimicking Jekyll's style. The way the final chapter is placed in authorial limbo again places evil beyond categorisation: if one is unsure which voice belongs to Hyde, it becomes impossible to categorise his words. As a result, while evil, through Hyde, is variously presented as an insatiable force, an instance of comic absurdity, and a hideous aesthetic, it is ultimately portrayed as all of these things and none: a concept beyond delineation."

A portrait of the revolutionary Nineteenth Century biologist, Charles Darwin (1809-1882).

ESSAY PLAN SEVEN

READ THE FOLLOWING EXTRACT FROM CHAPTER 10 (HENRY JEKYLL'S FULL STATEMENT OF THE CASE) OF THE STRANGE CASE OF DR JEKYLL AND MR HYDE AND THEN ANSWER THE QUESTION THAT FOLLOWS.

I n this extract, Dr Jekyll recounts the first occasion he involuntarily morphs into Mr Hyde.

Some two months before the murder of Sir Danvers, I had been out for one of my adventures, had returned at a late hour, and woke the next day in bed with somewhat odd sensations. It was in vain I looked about me; in vain I saw the decent furniture and tall proportions of my room in the square; in vain that I recognised the pattern of the bed-curtains and the design of the mahogany frame; something still kept insisting that I was not where I was, that I had not wakened where I seemed to be, but in the little room in Soho where I was accustomed to sleep in the body of Edward Hyde. I smiled to myself, and, in my psychological way began lazily to inquire into the elements of this illusion, occasionally, even as I did so, dropping back into a comfortable morning doze. I was still so engaged when, in one of my more wakeful moments, my eyes fell upon my hand.

Now the hand of Henry Jekyll (as you have often remarked) was professional in shape and size: it was large, firm, white, and comely. But the hand which I now saw, clearly enough, in the yellow light of a mid-London morning, lying half shut on the bed-clothes, was lean, corded, knuckly, of a dusky pallor and thickly shaded with a swart growth of hair. It was the hand of Edward Hyde.

I must have stared upon it for near half a minute, sunk as I was in the mere stupidity of wonder, before terror woke up in my breast as sudden and startling as the crash of cymbals; and bounding from my bed, I rushed to the mirror. At the sight that met my eyes, my blood was changed into something exquisitely thin and icy. Yes, I had gone to bed Henry Jekyll, I had awakened Edward Hyde. How was this to be explained? I asked myself, and then, with another bound of terror—how was it to be remedied?

Starting with this extract, how does Stevenson present Dr Jekyll as unable to control Mr Hyde?

Write about:

• **how Stevenson presents Dr Jekyll as unable to control Mr Hyde in this extract.**

• **how Stevenson presents Dr Jekyll as unable to control Mr Hyde in the novel as a whole.**

Introduction

"Perhaps the biggest intellectual upheaval in Nineteenth Century life was brought about by Sigmund Freud's psychoanalytic theories, which revolutionized how humans saw themselves: Freud perceived existence as a struggle between, on one hand, our base instinct (the "Id"), and, on the other, those forces that check and moderate our urges (the "Ego" and "Super Ego"). In this curious passage – which narrates an episode in Hyde's existence, yet seemingly from Jekyll's point of view – Stevenson explores the tussle for power between the ravenous Hyde and the moderate Jekyll, and, in so doing, arguably dramatises this Freudian inner struggle."

Theme/Paragraph One: Stevenson uses sleep in this passage to communicate Hyde's dominance over Jekyll: not only does the dream's contents reflect this dominance, but the very act of sleeping itself – a state in which one is powerless to control one's thoughts – hints at the empowerment of baser instincts.

- The first section of this passage explores how the dozing Hyde, despite the physical evidence that he is in Jekyll's home – he intermittently glimpses 'the decent furniture and tall proportions of my room in the square' – instead finds himself inhabiting an illusory mental recreation of Hyde's bedroom: 'I seemed to be... in the little room in Soho where I was accustomed to sleep in the body of Edward Hyde.' The way the Soho room has colonised the narrator's dozing mental space demonstrates the increasing dominion of Hydian thought. Indeed, the way the decor of the two rooms reflects Jekyll and Hyde physically – the 'tall proportions' versus the 'little room in Soho' – gives extra clarity to the significance of the one room supplanting the other in this dream. Indeed, the reader is about to learn that Hyde has quite literally supplanted Jekyll without the use of the potion for the first time. The dream-conjured bedroom foreshadows this fact. [*AO1 for advancing the argument with judiciously selected quotes; AO2 for the close analysis of the language*].

- It ought to be noted that the very fact Hyde is sleeping is important, since, in Freud's formulation, sleep is a state in which the conscious mind surrenders control and the baser instincts (the "Id") are given free expression. As a result, sleep itself is a symbol of Hyde's dominance over Jekyll. [*AO3 for providing insightful historical-philosophical context*].

- *Elsewhere in the novel*: Sleep is used elsewhere in the novel to express the increasing power of Hyde over others. For instance, in chapter two, Utterson experiences frenzied dreams about Hyde, as Hyde comes to dominate Utterson's consciousness and unduly influences Utterson's decision-making

Theme/Paragraph Two: Although this passage features Hyde as opposed to Jekyll, the paralysing fear expressed by the Jekyllian inner-voice indicates a loss of control on Jekyll's part.

- Curiously, although this scene unequivocally revolves around Hyde – indeed, it is this fact that gives the scene its drama – one still registers a Jekyllian inner-voice: not simply Jekyll-the-narrator looking back in retrospect, but an inner-Jekyll who seems to be present in Hyde's mind as this event plays out. However, the key emotional state of this inner-Jekyll, as the realisation of the involuntary transition hits, is that of paralysing fear. At the start of the second paragraph, he is at first quite literally paralysed with fear: he was 'sunk in the sheer stupidity of wonder' – the paragraph break, combined with the meandering opening sentence of this paragraph, forcing the reader to pause to let this tableau sink in. The inner-Jekyll then experiences a 'terror' waking 'in [his] breast' that was as 'startling as the crash of cymbals,' and his blood 'chang[ing] into something exquisitely thin and icy.' [*AO1 for advancing the argument with judiciously selected quotes; AO2 for the close analysis of the language and for discussing how form shapes meaning*].

- The sheer fear experienced by the inner-Jekyll, and the paralysis it induces, implicitly indicates Jekyll's weakness in relation to Hyde: he is so struck with fear that he is unable to act to bring Hyde in line. *Elsewhere in the novel*: That fear can be a crippling force in the novel is made evident by the case of Lanyon, whose intense horror in the face of Hyde's transformation to Jekyll in fact proves lethal.

Theme/Paragraph Three: The symbolism of the hand is important in this passage, since it strongly

hints at Jekyll's increasing lack of control over Hyde.

- The stimuli that precipitates Hyde/the inner-Jekyll's realisation that there has been involuntary night-time transition is the sight of a hand: whereas the narrator remarks that he had expected to see Jekyll's 'large, firm, white' hand, he instead encountered Hyde's 'lean, corded, knuckly' extremity. Given that hands are a potent symbol of man's ability to exert control over his environment, the disappearance of Jekyll's hand is a symbol of his loss of control over Hyde: Hyde quite literally has the upper hand. [*AO1 for advancing the argument with judiciously selected quotes*].

- However, the observation that 'it was the hand of Edward Hyde' – a remark given structural emphasis as a result of it appearing at the paragraph's close – seems to contain a secret double meaning: it invites the reader to consider the possibility that the entirety of the final chapter might have been written by the hand of Edward Hyde; after all, Hyde's handwriting matches Jekyll's, and Hyde apes Jekyll's style in his letter to Lanyon. By hinting at this possibility, Stevenson further nods to Jekyll's loss of control: there is a chance that he has been robbed of his chance to give his own narrative, and thus has lost utter control of the story. [*AO2 for the close analysis of the language*].

Theme/Paragraph Four: Although the inner-Jekyll is portrayed as horrified in this passage, his mere

presence while Hyde is at large suggests that Jekyll still possesses no small sway over proceedings.

- Although the reader is encountering Hyde in this passage, there is still (as has been mentioned) a kind of inner-Jekyll present. While this inner-Jekyll is paralysed by fear during this extract's denouement, there is also evidence that this inner-Jekyll's intelligence still persists, and this intelligence itself functions as a tacit rebuke to Hyde's authority. For instance, one might dissect the following remark: 'in my psychological way [I] began lazily to inquire into the elements of this illusion.' Not only is the act of self reflection and the scholarly vocabulary ('psychological' and 'inquire') what one would expect from Jekyll, but it also demonstrates how firmly lodged in place the inner-Jekyll remains. Indeed, even the paralysing fear exhibited by Jekyll in this passage can be construed as a rebuke to Hyde's authority: it hints at a persistent moral code that is at odds with Hyde's modus operandi. [*AO1 for advancing the argument with judiciously selected quotes; AO2 for the close analysis of the language*].

- *Elsewhere in the novel*: The inner-Jekyll is shown to exercise significant control over Hyde in the action proceeding this extract. The inner-Jekyll's repeated efforts to galvanise Hyde to transform himself back to Jekyll, though unsuccessful, hint that Jekyll's moral repulsion towards Hyde remains at all times more potent than Hyde's desire to exist.

Conclusion

On this occasion, I am integrating literary criticism into the conclusion. As it so happens, though it'll likely score AO3 marks, literary criticism is more something that examiners expect from A Level students, and even the top band GCSE students should not be worrying about including it. However, it was just so dang relevant that I couldn't resist. Also, because Chesterton was writing very shortly after Stevenson, his observations could arguably be categorised as literary context.

"G. K. Chesterton noted that the real stab of Stevenson's story is not that one man is two men, but that two men are one man; after all, they fail to exist as two separate entities: when one dies, they both die. As a result, the premise of this question might be considered a non-sequitur, for Jekyll and Hyde are the same man.[1] It makes more sense to see them as warring parts of one mind: the animal Hyde (the "Id") versus the civilised Jekyll (the "Ego" and "Super Ego"). That the Hydian base instincts eventually get the upper hand is undeniable: Stevenson demonstrates this through the symbolism of dreams and Hyde's hands. Yet the end product of this inner conflict does not appear to be Hydian dominance so much as mutually assured destruction."

A portrait of Sigmund Freud (1856-1939),
the highly influential father of
psychoanalysis.

NOTES

ESSAY PLAN ONE

1. The Irish Fenians were fighting for independence from British rule and were outsiders insofar as they were outlaws who engaged in terrorist activities.

   Homosexual acts between men were illegal right up until 1967, the year which saw the passing of the Sexual Offences Act – the legislation that decriminalized homosexuality in the UK.

2. 'Cum' in 'Jekyll-cum-Hyde' is a Latin phrase. It is usually used to describe two characteristics about a certain individual – for example, Barack Obama is a lawyer-cum-politician.

   Of course, the situation with regards to Jekyll and Hyde is somewhat more complex. However, as G. K. Chesterton observed in his fantastic essay on the novel, 'the real stab of the story is not the discovery that the one man is two men; but in the discovery that the two men are one man.' He then observes that when one dies, both die – that is, ultimately there is always just 'one man born and only one man buried.' As a result, when I write Jekyll-cum-Hyde, it is an acknowledgement that these two men are ultimately one man, and it is thus a useful technique to allow me to discuss this hybrid individual.

   If you're curious, you can read more of Chesterton's essay at the following URL:

   http://platitudesundone.blogspot.com/2010/09/jekyll-and-hyde.html

3. "Précis" is a French word that has entered the English language. It means a summary.

4. An epigraph is a short quote at the beginning of a work of literature that hints at the themes and concepts that will be discussed.

5. To transgress means to go beyond the limits, and is often used to describe behaviour that goes either beyond the law or beyond moral conduct. However, we can also talk about physical transgressions – that is, when someone gains entry to a forbidden space.

6. The word doppelgänger is in fact German and it is kind of like a spooky double. However, the doppelgänger doesn't necessarily have to be a physical double. It could instead reflect some other characteristic in the person in question.

7. The word eponymous is used to describe a situation in which the title of a text is named after the main character.

8. Laissez-faire is a French expression which has entered English usage. It means "to leave alone."

9. The mise-en-page – yet another French expression! – refers to the way the text appears on the page.

ESSAY PLAN TWO

1. A phallus refers to an erect penis. A phallic object is an object that is reminiscent – and perhaps even represents – an erect penis.
2. The word "Freudian" refers to the father of psychoanalysis, Sigmund Freud (1856 – 1939). His works explore the hidden sexual motivations that drive human beings. When we are doing a Freudian reading of a text, we are looking for the hidden sexual imagery – imagery that perhaps even the author themselves had not realised had possessed sexual undertones.

   Freud was operating at the end of the Nineteenth Century, and his works had a palpable impact on the artistic output of the time.
3. If something is histrionic, it is dramatic in nature – perhaps even *overly* dramatic in nature.

ESSAY PLAN FOUR

1. Horace Walpole's *The Castle of Otranto* (1764) is considered the first ever Gothic novel. He claimed he found the manuscript in his attic, and that it was originally written during the Crusades – which was, of course, hokum!

ESSAY PLAN FIVE

1. On February 26, 1884, Fenian terrorists dynamited a cloakroom within Victoria Station. The attack on Scotland Yard – also by Fenian terrorists – took place on May 30 of the same year.
2. Aural refers to how things sound.

ESSAY PLAN SEVEN

1. Non-sequitur is a Latin phrase and means 'does not follow.' I'm basically arguing that the question, by framing Jekyll and Hyde as separate individuals, does not make sense!

AFTERWORD

To keep up to date with Accolade Press, visit https://
accoladetuition.com/accolade-press. You can also join our
private Facebook group (where our authors share resources and
guidance) by visiting the following link: https://rcl.ink/DME.

Printed in Great Britain
by Amazon